Mind Hack Your Golf

Improve Your Game

Margaret Potter, PhD

Copyright © 2018 Margaret Potter. All rights reserved.

No part of this publication may be reproduced, distributed, or transmitted in any form or by any means, including photocopying, recording, or other electronic or mechanical methods, without the prior written permission of the publisher, except in the case of brief quotations embodied in reviews and certain other non-commercial uses permitted by copyright law.

ISBN: 9780648451204

Dedication

I dedicate this book to my family who inspire me to become the best I can be.

Ko toku kaha me taku angitu e tika ana ki taku whanau

My strength and success are due to my family.

Table of Contents

Foreword 7
Preface 11
Introduction 15

Section 1: Preparation: Create the Right Headspace 17
    Growth versus fixed mindset 18
    Self-belief 22
    Self-discipline 25
    Set SMART goals 26
    Summary 31
    REFLECTIVE QUESTIONS 32

Section 2: Practice: Build Your Mind Muscle 33
    How do you learn best? 34
    Mindfulness 39
    Concentration 42
    Self-talk 48
    Imagery 53
    Summary 61
    REFLECTIVE QUESTIONS 62

Section 3: Performance: Let It Happen 63
    How does your mind work? 64
    Building self-trust 67
    Skill development 71
    Accepting your mistakes 76
    Summary 79
    REFLECTIVE QUESTIONS 80

Section 4: Pursuit: Enjoyment and Success 81
　　Positive psychology 82
　　Positive emotions 85
　　Building character 90
　　A strengths-based approach 96
　　Summary 99
　　REFLECTIVE QUESTIONS 101
Section 5: Progress: Quality Versus Quantity 102
　　The Keep It Simple Seriously (KISS) principle 103
　　Deliberate practice 107
　　Continuous Quality Improvement (CQI) 112
　　Summary 116
　　REFLECTIVE QUESTIONS 117

Conclusion 119
End Notes 121
Acknowledgments 123

Foreword

I have known Margaret on a professional level as her coach and mentor for the past 5+ years. Before we started a program in 2013, I asked Margaret what her goal was and she replied, "To become the best golfer I can be." It was at this point I sensed that with her attitude she could become very good at the game.

We started working together and after a few months of coaching she decided she would join the Royal Fremantle Golf Club to take her game further. At this point, her progress to becoming a low single figure player in just a few years is, in my opinion quite an accomplishment. Not only did Margaret achieve this as a mature-aged student, but she has also had to overcome physical limitations including:

- Permanent loss of feeling in her right lower limb due to past major spinal surgery. This particularly affects weight transfer and balance.

- The inability to properly bend her middle and ring fingers due to past fractures to her right hand. This affects one of the most critical basic fundamentals of the game—"the grip."

It wasn't until sometime into our relationship that I learnt more about Margaret and her academic background and qualifications. So, as part of my coaching methodology I asked her to diarize significant learning points that have helped her develop her game.

Below are examples of those entries:

1. **Logical approach.** Keep everything as simple as possible.

2. **Get information in a way that works for me.** I need to develop my knowledge to a level that ensures I can self-analyze and self-manage as part of my own practice and performance.

3. **Focus on getting the basics right.** This includes grip, posture, alignment. I recognize the importance of the fundamentals and continue to be a work-in-progress—vigilance is required!

4. **Practice is practice and playing is playing.** Never mix these two up, especially during a competition. Work out how to play with the game I bring on a particular day—good, bad or ugly! This has helped me become more patient; to try hard as if it doesn't matter (swing freely even if I make mistakes); to be more creative and a better problem-solver when on the course.

5. **Get a good understanding of the mechanics of the golf swing.** Appreciate what I am supposed to be doing and leverage off my knowledge and ability in one area to develop my confidence and skills in other areas.

By getting Margaret to do this, it has helped me to better understand how her mind works, which in turn has enhanced our communication and understanding. In this book you will find a variety of tools and tips to help you achieve your goals, not only for the game of golf but, also in the game of life.

Robert (Henry) Stevens

PGA Australia

Preface

There are lots and lots of books describing the importance of mental skills for golf performance. So much so that initially I wondered whether it would be worthwhile to write one more. What would my angle of attack be? What could I offer that wasn't already out there?

After considerable time observing and listening to how other golfers manage the mental challenges of the game, it became apparent that what I take for granted in terms of applying a systematic mental skills approach is well worth sharing. I recognized that if I could help others identify ways to better manage themselves they could also learn to 'mind hack' their golf. This was affirmed when I started working as a mind coach with up-and-coming golfers as well as elite ones. I noticed that from a psychological perspective, they are a welcoming receptacle for information and have so much untapped potential.

In four and a half years of playing the game, I have developed an absolute passion for it. Since I began, I've progressed from a novice to a low single figure golfer. To appreciate what I have to offer, it is worthwhile to reflect on where I've come from in life, not just in golf.

For more than 25 years I have been helping people in all walks of life become the best version of themselves. This started out in the physical domain when I completed degrees in physical education and physiotherapy in New Zealand and worked in injury rehabilitation. This transitioned to assisting people in the psychological domain when I came to Perth in Western Australia to complete a Master's Degree in Sport Psychology and a Doctor of Philosophy (PhD) focused on communication in health.

In my early thirties, I was confronted with a life changing event. Unexpectedly, I found myself in a Spinal Injury Unit with Cauda Equina Syndrome, secondary to a central disc protrusion. The worst thing was that I had to undergo spinal surgery twice and have been left with permanent spinal damage. The best thing is that I have used the experience to develop an extremely resilient and powerful mind. Without a doubt, this has become my greatest asset in both my work and leisure pursuits.

Based on my knowledge, skills, life, and golf experience thus far, I know this book has something to offer to anyone who wants to improve their game. I'm 100 percent confident about this because I've consistently used the skills to advance my own game and received a great deal of positive feedback from my clients about the beneficial strategies that I share in this book.

I'm hoping the book will appeal to men, women, and children of all ages and abilities. In essence, it has been written for anyone who wants to improve their mental skills. Your goal may be to drop 5 to 10 shots off your handicap, regularly shoot in the low 70s or 80s in club play, or successfully turn professional. It's up to you to determine what you want and how hard you're prepared to work for it, but I would be delighted if this book were to play a small part on your journey.

Keep enjoying the great game!

All the best,

Margaret Potter, PhD

September 2018

Introduction

Golf is a very rewarding yet endlessly frustrating game. When you play a round of golf, there is a huge amount of time available for your mind to wander. It wouldn't be so bad if you could quickly get your mind back on track, but how often do you find that you mess things up in the critical moments like when you take your club to the top of the backswing, or when you are about to execute a really close putt to shoot a great score? Despite the feelings of fear and failure that can overwhelm you like a fast approaching storm, many a golf tragic will keep rocking up to the course each week to subject themselves to more of the same.

How would you like to take charge of your mind and play your golf on your own terms? What would you be willing to sacrifice for a higher level of consistency that allowed you to perform better on demand? This book is for people who know they can do better and who want more from their game. It provides a holistic approach with key ingredients that can help you to create your own great golf mind. Every time you prepare to play a game or plan to execute a shot, you'll have the tools to organize your thinking and use your mind purposefully to help you achieve your goals.

The game of golf is full of *should have-, could have-,* and *would have*-but-didn't stories! For example, when your golf partner slams their driver into their bag after wildly hooking their ball off the tee into the rough and declares, "I knew I *should* have used my 3-wood off the tee because something about this hole always just does my head in." Or after you skull your chip shot through the green and say to yourself, "I *could* have used my putter and just got it up there close to the hole. What was I thinking?" Or you overhear a conversation back in the clubhouse when a player is recounting a missed short putt on the 18th to birdie the hole and says, "I *would* normally back myself to hole that putt every day of the week, but not today."

Don't be the golfer who laments what might have been and instead learn how to act with foresight. Be the 'go to' golfer in match play that your teammates know will get the job done. Take control of your destiny and be the kind of person who acts with purpose on every shot and confidently deals with the consequences, whatever they may be. Be the kind of person who when facing adversity stands tall and smiles because you trust in your ability and love the opportunity to rise to the challenge.

The tips, tricks, and strategies in this book will provide a solid platform for you to create your own mind mastery. All you have to do is apply the information to your game. If you want to gain better control of your mind on the golf course, I urge you to read on.

Section I
Preparation: Create the Right Headspace

"Success depends almost entirely on how effectively you learn to manage the game's two ultimate adversaries: the course and yourself."

—Jack Nicklaus

This section lays the foundations for improving how you think and act when playing golf. To do this we will work through some key ingredients that are fundamental to developing the mindset of a champion. The first step is to build your awareness of a range of characteristics that are critical to developing your mental capability. However, before you can effectively do that you need to get yourself into the right headspace.

GROWTH VERSUS FIXED MINDSET

Elite athletes recognize the importance of the mind. Tiger Woods, winner of 14 majors and the player with the most weeks at number one in the Official World Golf Rankings (683 weeks), has stated, "My mind is my biggest asset." Serena Williams, holder of 23 major singles tennis titles has alluded to the importance of her mind when she said, "Hang on to the thought of what you want. Make it absolutely clear." Roger Federer holder of 20 major singles titles has stated, "I'm a very positive thinker, and I think that is what helps me the most in difficult moments." Similarly, Usain Bolt, gold medalist in both the 100m and 200m events at three consecutive Olympics and considered the greatest sprinter in history, is quoted as saying, "Learning the mind is as important as understanding the body."

To optimize your potential, you need a growth rather than a fixed mindset. Carol Dweck, a Stanford University psychologist, described a fixed mindset as being something that one believes they can't really change. An individual with a fixed mindset tends to believe their ability to learn or achieve is set in stone and will measure their ability according to their success or failure at a given task. I often hear this on the golf course with comments like:

- "I'll never be able to lower my handicap."
- "I'm too old to learn a new way to swing the club."
- "Unless I spend hours and hours each week practicing, I won't improve."

An individual with a growth mindset attributes a great deal of value to effort and does not have a singular focus on the outcome. I sometimes hear these views on the golf course, but sadly, not nearly as often as those with a fixed mindset. Some of the comments I have heard include:

- "I didn't score that well today, but my focus was good, and I worked really hard on getting rid of self-doubt."
- "I was happy with my commitment to the difficult shots I played out of the rough. They didn't all come off, but I was clear about what I was trying to do and sometimes pulled it off."
- "I realize my success in golf is not about the good shots I play, but more about how I deal with the poor shots."

The belief that we can improve ourselves through effort and that one's true potential is not known are fundamental in an individual who has a growth mindset. He/she will have a passion for learning rather than a hunger for approval. These individuals will not be discouraged by failure; instead, they will use it as a key driver to future success. Michael Jordan, a member of the Chicago Bulls team that won six National Basketball Association (NBA) championship titles, and was winner of the NBA most valuable player award five times, illustrates what it means to have a growth mindset, "I've missed more than 9000 shots in my career. I've lost almost 300 games. Twenty-six times, I've been trusted to take the game-winning shot and missed. I've failed over and over and over again in my life. And that is why I succeed."

If you have a growth mindset, you never put a ceiling on the degree to which you can improve. To develop this type of mindset, you should:

1. **Pay attention to what you say to yourself (your inner talk).** Always choose to see your potential. Look for any specific learning that you can take away from your mistakes. For example, when you hit a poor shot let your internal dialogue be "I can do better" rather than "'I'm an idiot."

2. **Avoid openly talking down about yourself (your outer talk).** For a lot of golfers this negative talk is used as a pressure release valve, but it is an unhelpful approach. All it does is draw attention to your shortcomings. Your outburst will usually compel your playing partners to comfort or console you. This can

undermine your confidence because it negates your control of your game. This negative energy can also put others off their game, especially if it goes on for the entire round as it makes it harder for others to concentrate. This behavior can drain away positive energy, a bit like having oxygen sucked out of a room—not fun!

Even worse, if you openly talk down about yourself in a match play situation you are giving your opponent a potential advantage. They may not take it, but if they do, your match will be lost in your head long before it is over in reality. You are giving your opponent motivation and building their confidence, while diminishing your own. Sadly, if you do realize the error of your ways, you are likely to beat yourself up even more with negative inner talk, "How stupid am I?" or "Shut up you idiot." The best option is to avoid this situation in the first place.

3. **Give yourself an attitude transplant.** In the words of Maya Angelou (1928-2014), poet, singer, and activist, "If you don't like something change it. If you can't change it then change your attitude." This is particularly relevant if you have arrived at this point and are saying to yourself, "I appreciate what has been stated thus far, but I can't change who I am, or control how I respond to things, especially when I'm under pressure." This is the thinking of someone with a fixed

mindset. If you want to optimize your potential and have fun along the way, shift your focus of attention from the outcome to the process. Willingly take yourself on what may at times be a difficult journey and be amazed at just how informative and fun it can be.

SELF-BELIEF

Self-belief is essential to your success! If you are not your #1 supporter in whatever you are doing, how can you expect to excel? Self-belief encompasses who you are as a person, what your values are, what your history is, how you relate to people, and what you appreciate in yourself.

Sometimes when I'm out playing golf I notice a lack of self-belief in one or more of my playing partners. It comes through in what they say as well as their non-verbal behavior. They may disparage their game, technique, decision-making, and so on. In doing so, they choose to shine a big spotlight on their ineptitude. I've never met anyone who can consistently excel at anything when they do not back themselves to succeed.

You might say, "I am just giving myself a 'kick in the pants' to spur me into action," or "It's not that bad. I don't actually listen to what I'm saying. I just say stuff to get my frustration out." If this is your normal process, I urge you to rethink it. While you may notice some short-term improvement, it will not be sustainable. The more you beat yourself up, the less confidence you will have when it really matters (e.g., when you have to hit the next shot out of the rough or have to hit a ball from a bad lie in a bunker). When you lack confidence on the golf course, it translates into being indecisive, lacking commitment, and losing your form and technique with shots. All of these actions demonstrate a focus on the outcome of the shot instead of the process.

When you lose self-belief and confidence, you are bound to lose enjoyment. The less enjoyment you experience, the less motivation you will have. Your whole game will begin to spiral downward, and you end up with a self-fulfilling prophecy that might look something like this:

Every time you play a poor shot, you chastise yourself. It starts to happen more and more. And before you know it, you give up and are resigned to finishing with a poor score.

To play consistently well requires effort, persistence, and underlying this is self-belief. To build your bedrock of self-belief, consider doing one or more of the following activities:

1. **Choose an area for improvement and aim to make it a strength.** Every day say to yourself, "I'm going to

make this area (e.g., my putting, my chipping, my drives) the strongest part of my game."

2. **Accept the challenge and see it as interesting, even exciting.** Look forward to the journey of improvement. Every day say to yourself "How much am I going to learn and improve when I develop (my putting, my chipping, my drives, etc.)? It is going to be awesome!"

3. **Speak to yourself with kindness and compassion.** This is especially important because we all make mistakes. When you are working to improve in a particular area, you will get frustrated because your game may initially go backwards. You may temporarily lose faith. At times like these, say to yourself "Good effort," "Keep working on it," or "I can do this." Choose to pump yourself up—don't rob yourself of the energy and enthusiasm to face the challenge.

4. **Overcome limiting beliefs.** Your inner talk may be: "I'm not a good driver of the ball because I'm not flexible enough," "I can't chip to save my life," or "I always mess up close putts." If you allow limiting beliefs to invade your mind during practice or performance, your fate will be sealed. If you identify a limiting belief about yourself or your game, then set out to eliminate it. This will provide you with an exciting challenge to work on. Imagine the euphoric

feeling you will have when you manage to prove yourself wrong.

SELF-DISCIPLINE

To reach your full potential, you need to train your mind and body to the level of your performance expectations. If you want to be a golf professional, it will be essential to have a solid foundation of both physical and mental skills from which you can develop your overall game. If you are an amateur golfer playing once or twice a week for fun, you are likely to be satisfied with limited practice and will focus on playing. Regardless of level, everyone has expectations of how they want to play. We all aspire to do well.

The fact is that the older we get, the harder we have to work to maintain and improve our physical capabilities. However, on the mental side of things, our potential is often greater when we are older. With age our priorities shift, perhaps from a keen golf focus as a youngster, to our studies, then to work, career, and family commitments. This has an impact on our available time and motivation.

On the upside, a busy person is often a highly productive person who exhibits self-discipline. This means the individual is often well organized, likes to set goals and will apply him/herself with a great deal of focus and commitment. The big bonus with getting older is there is often a level of wisdom present that was not so evident when younger, and that can help you to think and act smart.

Spending quality time to train your mind can be the catalyst that makes a major difference because your mind has so much potential for improvement. Irrespective of age, in as little as 5 minutes per day of focused mind training, you can make a significant difference. However, there are two non-negotiable requirements to give yourself the best chance of success:

1. You must commit to working on a particular mental skill for at least 4 to 6 weeks to harvest your gains.
2. You must apply self-discipline to your mind training. Without it, you will easily get distracted and potentially lose sight of your goals. The mind is good at wandering if we allow it.

Set SMART Goals

Goal setting is a technique that can help you to identify clear targets for training and performance in any sport, or area of your life. Regarding a sport, your goals may have:

- a physical focus, such as improving aspects of general fitness, core strength, power, and flexibility.

- a technical or skill-based focus, such as perfecting a particular movement pattern in your golf swing or putting stroke.

- a nutritional focus, such as monitoring your food and fluid intake.

- a mental or behavioral focus that might involve the consistent application of positive self-talk, confident body language, or pre-shot imagery.

Types of goals

There are three main types of goals, but they are interconnected. Here are the types, along with descriptions and examples.

1. **Outcome goals.** These relate to achieving a specific result and are generally not under your full control. It is helpful to look at these as longer-term, big picture goals that will most likely take one or more years to achieve.

Examples of outcome goals include:

- Attain a single figure handicap by the end of the calendar year.

- Be selected to represent your club or state this year.

- Win a gold medal at the Olympics.

2. **Performance goals.** These relate to those self-imposed benchmarks that help you reach your outcome goal. Setting benchmarks or targets and recording your statistics can help you measure your effort toward achievement of performance goals.

Examples of performance goals include:

- Hit at least 75 percent of fairways off the tee per round.

- Reach at least 65 percent of greens in regulation.

- Average 30 putts per round.

If your outcome goal is to become a low, single-figure golfer and/or to turn professional, you will benefit from drilling down even further with your statistics, including both physical and mental performance goals.

From a mental perspective, this could include things like eliminating negative self-talk and demonstrating positive body language throughout a round, or sharpening your imagery so the picture you imagine for each shot has visual, auditory, and kinesthetic elements.

If you need assistance, your coach or a mentor will be able to help you to identify appropriate performance goals. Make sure you record your statistics in a notebook or electronically using a spreadsheet template or a free app. This allows you to monitor your progress, and if necessary, to adjust your performance goal(s).

3. **Process goals.** These are closely related to performance goals but are within your control. They represent the small steps you need to take to achieve both performance goals, and ultimately your outcome goals.

Examples of process goals include:

- Spend 1 hour, twice a week working on swing technique with long irons and woods.

- Spend 1 hour each week working on putting technique.

- Develop a simple and reliable pre-shot routine that includes both mental and physical cues.

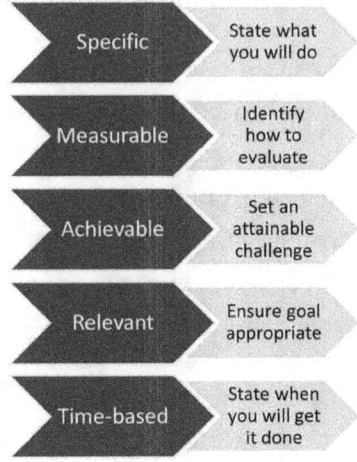

Figure 1: SMART Goal Setting Framework

While all three types of goals are important and provide a framework to motivate and guide you toward achievement, process and performance goals should be your primary focus on a day-to-day basis. These types of goals will provide you with feedback on your progress and should be documented using the SMART goal setting framework. SMART stands for:

Specific. You need to be able to clearly articulate what you want to achieve. This simplifies evaluation of your performance. Some useful questions to ask yourself include:

- What is my big picture goal? (outcome goal)

- What do I want to achieve today? this week? this month? (performance goals)

- What specific things do I need to work on to improve in each particular area of my game? (process goals)

Measurable. You should decide what you will measure to track goal attainment. This could include what you will see, hear, and feel when you reach your goal. If your outcome goal was to be selected onto a particular team, then the measure is self-evident. For process and performance goals, you can control what you will focus on, and that can help you determine what to measure.

Achievable. Think about where you are now, where you would like to be, and how much time you are prepared to commit. Then set your goals accordingly. Discussion with those who support you, like your coach, mentor, parents, or partner, can be helpful to ensure the goals you set are realistic and achievable.

Relevant. The goal needs to be important enough to ensure your commitment. There is no point in setting a process goal based on your swing pattern if you are not prepared to do the work required to modify your swing.

Time-based. By setting a timeframe for achievement, you have a defined period to work on your goal and a specific point in time to measure it. This can be used to motivate your practice and performance. It can also provide you with feedback that can inform you of the need to modify one or more of your goals.

Summary

In this section we have explored the importance of having a growth mindset, along with self-belief and self-discipline. These fundamentals will provide you with a solid foundation and enable you to set challenging but realistic goals, ensuring you make the best use of your time.

Everyone has the potential for improvement. Your capacity to achieve the goals you set will not only be influenced by your level of effort and commitment, but also your ability to enjoy the journey and 'hang in there,' particularly when the going gets tough.

REFLECTIVE QUESTIONS

Based on this section's information, you may find it helpful to write down some answers to the following questions:

1. How can I ensure that I bring and maintain a growth mindset in golf?

2. When I face adversity, what will I do to ensure I remain my #1 supporter?

3. What is my main priority in terms of an outcome goal?

4. Based on my outcome goal, what performance and process goals would be appropriate in the next 3, 6, 9, or 12 months?

5. Who can help me with my goal setting?

Section 2
Practice: Build Your Mind Muscle

"The road to success is always under construction."

—Arnold Palmer

Mastering any skill takes time and practice, and building your mind muscle is no exception. The purpose of this section is to introduce you to some specific mental skills that will assist you in organizing and managing your thoughts (especially the unhelpful ones) when playing golf. However, we will start off by exploring how you learn best. With that information you can identify creative ways to adapt or apply the skills we will cover that suit your individual needs.

How do you learn best?

If you want to make the most of your potential, it makes sense to understand how you learn and what works best for you. The better you know yourself, the more successful you will be at learning from others and coaching yourself. Let's consider the following scenario as it may provide you with some insight into your learning preferences on the golf course:

> You are playing a short par 4 and have arrived at your ball to play your second shot. You have chosen a 6-iron and decided on the shot you will play. You remove the club from your bag and are in the process of moving towards your ball to get set up for your shot.

An individual who is readily able to see the shot in their mind, as if watching a video, is likely to have a *visual preference*. This may be very strong and enable them to see a high level of detail with the ability to pause and rewind the video on demand, or it may be less developed, so they can only see the target. Given that a picture is worth a thousand words, those with a high visual preference are often quick talkers and will be quick to action. This may mean they fail to take adequate time to plan and decide before they act, or they may find they often swing their club too fast because of the natural tendency to do everything quickly.

For those with a high visual preference, it will take a lot of conscious effort to slow everything down, including their breathing, swing, and walking pace. However, if they get in the habit of doing so, the result can be significant improvement in shot execution and enjoyment of the game.

An individual who likes to talk to him/herself as part of their routine and is acutely aware of the sound of ball contact, more so than ball flight, is likely to have an *auditory preference*. This will be unhelpful if external noises or one's inner voice easily distract them from the task at hand.

If one can focus on the positive value of an auditory preference, they can use aids like music during practice to help with relaxation. There are also freely available or paid apps that can assist with tempo. You could also create your own audio. This may be as simple as saying "one (ready), two (club to top of backswing), and three (execute)" in the right rhythm. Once an individual has developed comfort and confidence using audio cues in practice, they can work on reproducing the same emotional state on demand during competition.

An individual who likes to feel the club in their hands and responds to subtle changes in grip pressure, likes to move around to loosen up their arms, shoulders, head, and neck, or just can't resist waggling the club as they settle into their pre-shot routine is likely to have a *kinesthetic preference*. These often largely unconscious movements are all about getting comfortable and having the right physical feelings before executing the shot.

Those with a high kinesthetic preference will tend to be slower to walk to their ball and to play their shots. This is generally not because they have a conscious 'go slow' mentality. Instead, it is more reflective of their inner compass which derives joy from living, breathing, and feeling the experience. The fact these individuals can be in their own world can be a distinct advantage if they can draw on this ability when under pressure.

What does this mean for you and your golf? In reality, we are not all of one thing and none of the others. We are adaptable and exhibit commonalities. Ultimately, however, we are each wired in our own particular way. You will be a combination of all of the senses, and certainly if you can learn to bring them all to life in a meaningful way, you will derive significant benefits. Yet, most people will find one sensory domain will resonate most strongly when learning a new skill. This is apparent when you have a gut feeling or instinct about what works for you.

Think back to when you first learned to swing a golf club or when you first worked on your golf swing with a coach. As you were processing the information about what you saw, heard, and felt for the first time, how were you making sense of it? You may have found yourself saying things like:

- "Can you show me that again?"
- "I can see what you're saying in my mind."
- "It looks like I need to do this."

These are examples of the anchors associated with someone whose first preference is visual processing.

Alternatively, you may have found yourself saying things like:

- "Can you explain that again?"
- "Please talk me through it step-by-step."
- "It sounds like what I need to do is…"

These are examples of responses that highlight an auditory preference.

Or, you may have found yourself saying things like:

- "I need to work this out in my own time."
- "Can you put me in the right position and tell me what I should feel?"
- "Once I get a feel for it I know I'll be able to do it."

These comments reflect a kinesthetic preference, where taking one's time to get a feel for a movement is the preferred strategy.

Of course, as time goes by you will bring all of your senses to bear as you seek to maximize your learning. However, do not underestimate the value of clarity around your first preference, as this is an important signpost showing the best place to start. When you start with this preference, learning can often be augmented because you will pick up things quickly. It will also be the best point of focus to anchor more learning when you get stuck, confused, or overwhelmed.

By knowing yourself you can find a coach who works well with your dominant sensory preference. The best coaches will be able to teach things in different ways, so sometimes you can guide your coach on what works best for you and accelerate your learning from there.

The best thing is that knowledge is power, so by being able to affirm your strengths and more importantly identify your weaknesses, you can pinpoint both what you should work on and how you should work on it. This will allow you to establish routines that work to your strengths, while helping you maintain consistency, which is at the heart of the game of golf.

If you are interested to delve deeper into your sensory preferences, I would recommend you read more of the work by Neil Fleming and colleagues[1] who introduced the VARK questionnaire for assessing individual learning preferences in the visual, auditory, read/write, and kinesthetic modes. To work out your learning preferences, you can complete the VARK questionnaire for athletes at http://vark-learn.com/.

Mindfulness

Mindfulness is all about being in the present moment, becoming aware of your thoughts and feelings without judgement, and being able to let things go. A mindful golfer can readily tune in, act, and then deal with the consequences of their actions without becoming overly invested, freezing, or overreacting.

There is plenty of research indicating that the practice of mindfulness can have a beneficial impact on an individual's overall health and well-being. You may not immediately see how you can incorporate mindful practices into your game, so let's explore some ideas that you can work on.

1. **Practice mindful breathing**. Tune into your breath and feel the natural flow of air in and out. Become aware of how you are breathing. After a few in-out breaths you may notice your mind start to wander. This is quite normal, just gently redirect your mind back to your breathing.

If we consider your sensory preferences, those who have a strong kinesthetic preference are likely to love this activity and find it easy and helpful. Why? These individuals are often naturally nose (in), mouth (out) breathers and engage their diaphragm to get good distribution of air throughout their lungs. The pace of their relaxed breathing is slow and rhythmical allowing them time to focus on their breathing, and to feel the positive impact of the breath on their body.

This can be extremely helpful when distracted or feeling pressure as relaxed mindful breathing can act as an internal anchor on which to focus your attention.

Those with a visual preference tend to be more upper chest, shallow breathers, while those with an auditory preference breathe more to the mid-chest. Individuals with these two preferences may not find that the practice of relaxed breathing reduces their stress as well as other strategies do. However, it is not because the practice itself is unhelpful, but rather because it may not connect as easily with their natural strengths.

If you bring your growth mindset to the fore, variation in breathing patterns is not a problem, rather you are presented with an opportunity to work on an area to make it a strength. It would be beneficial to get into the habit of relaxed, controlled nose-mouth breathing. It would also be useful to get good quality air entry right down through your chest into the base of your lungs before letting it gently flow out of your mouth as you relax and exhale.

From a golf perspective, by using this technique, you learn how to better pace yourself. In addition, you will get more oxygen to your brain, helping you to take your time and make good decisions that contribute to effective course management.

2. **Practice mindful walking.** Tune in to your walking and pay attention to each step. What do you feel? Are you tight or relaxed? Are you balanced? Is there any discomfort? As the answers flow, just acknowledge them and let them go as you come back to focusing on each step.

Integrate your relaxed breathing practice with your walking. Become aware of your posture, the way you are carrying yourself and how it feels. Also notice what's going on around you—the noises, the people—but don't dwell on what you are seeing or hearing. Just acknowledge it and then come back to your pace and breath. Be in your own zone.

This mindful practice may be something you do as you walk from the carpark to the course, or between shots or holes. Mindful walking can be really helpful to get you 'out of your head' if you have got a lot going on outside of golf, or if you are overthinking your shots or feeling disappointed when out on the course.

If you commit yourself to improving mindfulness, over time it will help you with:

- handling the pressure felt with a crucial shot.
- letting go of anger and disappointment after poor shots.
- being able to narrowly focus your attention when you need to.
- improving your memory and decision-making ability.

Consider your natural tendencies to determine how mindful walking and/or breathing can best be incorporated into your game. The most obvious places to use mindfulness practices are pre-game for just a few minutes. This helps to settle your nerves and get you focused. You can also use mindful breathing pre-shot for 10-15 seconds to help you tune in, and post-shot for seconds to minutes as you accept the outcome and move on.

CONCENTRATION

When you watch the best golfers in the world it seems like they are easily able to concentrate on exactly the right things at the right time to get the right outcome. They can narrow their focus of attention quickly. They readily block out the distractions of the outside world while also controlling their inner thoughts. This helps them to execute shot after shot after shot with a high degree of precision. Such mastery may lull you into believing that doing so is easy, until the next time you go out to play. Consider this scenario:

> You are standing on the first tee with your playing partners, looking forward to a great day's golf. Some random thoughts enter your mind as you stand silently with your group. "I hope I shut the garage door" or "I must remember to go to the post office on my way home." Next you tap into your external environment and hear one of your playing partners complaining that they heard the ground staff are pruning trees beside the fairway on the second. Now you become aware of a sound in the distance and think to yourself "That's probably the ground staff with a chainsaw. They better not rev it up and put me off when I'm hitting!"

With all of these thoughts popping into your head, is it any surprise that when it is your turn to tee off and you try to pinpoint your focus to your shot, it is really difficult? The bottom line is that energy will flow to where your attention goes. If you are having lots of conscious thoughts that are either about the task, or completely unrelated to it, that will distract you from where your focus of attention needs to be. The result is that you end up paying attention to the wrong things at the wrong time. Maybe you are dwelling on the

3-putt you had two holes ago, or the personal best score you will achieve if you can par the next two holes. It is important to recognize that ruminating on the past or focusing on the future does not help you to be where we need you right now.

Bender and Mercier[2] studied the shot process of golf's greatest male champions. They suggest once a decision has been made and you have club in hand, your pre-shot routine should take 10-12 seconds. Then from the time you set your lead foot, step over the ball, and swing to the finish, you should take eight seconds. Bear in mind that a very small amount of that eight seconds will be your actual swing time.

Applying your full concentration to each shot takes a fraction of the total time for your round. However, putting solid routines in place and maintaining self-discipline for consistent execution of your shots, takes a lot of practice. Some tips to improve your concentration include:

1. **Ensure you stay hydrated when playing golf.** The body has an extremely high-water content, so if you get dehydrated, it can negatively impact on your mood, concentration, memory, decision-making ability, and overall endurance.

2. **Practice mindfulness techniques during your round**. This will help calm your mind and enable you to focus in the 'present moment' when you need to.

3. **Divide your routine into the following three distinct parts:**

    a. *Decision-making.* This can start when you have arrived at your ball (not before) and end when you have decided what you will do.

    b. *Pre-shot routine.* Identify a cue that signals your starting point. For example, if you take your glove on and off for every shot, it could be when you put it on, or you could start from the time you have the club for the shot in your hands and end when you are settled over the ball.

    c. *Shot routine.* This occurs from being settled over the ball until completion of your shot.

    The reason to break down a closely sequenced process into three components is to provide clarity to each of the parts. Part A (decision-making) is a conscious process, Part B (pre-shot) is a conscious/subconscious process, and Part C should be an unconscious process. Perhaps you are good at Part A but overthink Part C. Or you could take too long for Part A and then rush and become inconsistent with Part B. Breaking the routine down has the advantage of allowing you to closely evaluate and fine tune each part.

4. **Develop some physical and mental cues.** These should align with the three parts of your routine. This

will help you acquire a well-connected pattern of thoughts and actions that become ingrained.

For example, imagine you are playing a short par 4 and have driven the ball to a good position on the fairway. You have 130 yards (120 metres) to the flag.

Part A (decision-making). Use a physical cue (grabbing your rangefinder or tapping your thigh) and a mental cue like positive self-talk such as "I got this" or "Go to work." These actions should help you to focus on the task at hand.

Part B (pre-shot routine). Your physical cue may be having the club in both hands or standing behind the ball and looking down at the ground and up at the target once or twice and a mental cue could be "Bring it" or "Focus now." These actions should help you to narrow your attention even more.

Part C (shot routine). This part should be largely automated and is simply the action of making the shot. If you pause too long over the ball you can almost guarantee a poor outcome. You may have an unconscious trigger move (e.g., a waggle of the club, a re-grip of the club, a forward press with your hands) to start your action and at that point you should trust and execute. It would be helpful to get feedback on your shot routine from your coach or mentor so that you can develop good habits.

Make sure you come up with simple physical and mental cues that work for you. Don't be afraid to refine your cues over time as you get more in tune with yourself and your game. For example, after a lesson, you may want to consciously draw your attention to something you are working on that is helping your swing. Develop a physical cue word to help you to do that, such as "hip through" or "elbow in." Similarly, following a great round you may notice a word, phrase, or action helped you focus or control your emotions. If so, keep using it.

Your goal is to develop a simple, reliable process that you are confident to follow, especially when under pressure.

Figure 2: Keyword Cue Card

Another tip that I have found helpful when developing my routine is to carry a laminated card in my pocket with my keyword cues on it. If I get distracted, confused, or nervous, I can take it out and read it between shots. This helps me to refocus and anchors me to my routine.

SELF-TALK

Having multiple thoughts swirling around in your head is normal, albeit some people seem to have much more going in their internal 'black box' compared with others. When things go wrong on the golf course you may find your inner talk goes something like this: "I am such an idiot?" or "Don't mess this up too!" The reality is that if you don't take charge of your thinking, it will take charge of you.

Even when you play a great shot, you may find your dialogue goes something like this: "That was lucky," "I can't believe I pulled that off!", or "Thank goodness I didn't mess it up." While these are not strong negative remarks, neither are they confidence boosting.

To create a great golf mind and get the maximum benefit out of your self-talk, you need to be able to deal with a negative stream of consciousness. Work out how to call yourself to action in an unrelentingly positive (and even humorous) manner. In Section 1 we discussed the importance of self-belief and being your own #1 supporter; this is where positive self-talk has a critical role to play.

Occasional accolades in between many condemnations will most likely be insufficient; we tend to dwell in the negative space much more easily than the positive. For every bad thing you say to yourself, you'll have to say 10 times more positive things to level yourself out, and to be honest that takes more work than trying to diminish or eliminate negative self-talk.

We have already discussed how to integrate self-talk with physical cues into your golf routine. In addition, you can use self-talk at various times throughout a round of golf. For example, positive self-talk can help us recover from a poorly executed shot, bolster our confidence to perform a difficult shot, or help us to focus on executing a flawless process.

To expect you'll always adopt and maintain a positive mindset when playing golf is aspirational but unrealistic. So how do you measure up? Try the following activity, which aims to help you tune into self-talk.

> As you prepare for a competitive round of golf, take a new packet of 30 or more tees and place them in your right pocket. As your round of golf unfolds, every time you notice you have an unhelpful or negative thought in your head, transfer a tee from your right pocket to your back

pocket. How far do you progress around the course before you empty your right pocket?

Well done if you managed to keep the majority of tees in your right pocket for the entire round. However, it is more than likely that you fell short of that mark. As you start to work on controlling your self-talk, you can use this activity to check on improvement.

It is important to realize that there are unhelpful, unrelated thoughts that can impact on how you are thinking, feeling, and behaving when playing a round of golf. This might include thoughts related to stress at work, school, or home; financial issues; or physical or mental health problems. While positive self-talk is fundamentally important, so is having the ability to acknowledge and accept that some days you will struggle more than others. That is normal.

When things are not going well, show some self-compassion. Offer yourself the same level of support and comfort that you would to a close friend who was having problems. If you are having a particularly bad day and your game has fallen into a big black hole, appreciate that sometimes trying harder makes things worse, not better.

Apply a growth mindset and look for anything positive that you can take away. It may be that you have managed to maintain an A-grade attitude despite the poor score, or that you have been able to focus on one part of your game that was positive, or you have managed to control negative emotions using mindfulness activities and self-talk.

There are general and specific types of self-talk that can be used to assist an individual with concentration, building confidence, and supporting skill execution including:

1. **Instructional self-talk.** This is meant to focus your attention on a key component of a skill. For example, "down the line," "back and through," "good contact with the ball" when you are using your driver, woods, and irons, or "line and pace" related to your putting stroke.

2. **Motivational self-talk.** This is used to increase effort, manage anxiety, and provide encouragement. For example, "I've got this," "Come on," or "Breathe and relax."

To improve your self-talk, you can try one or more of the following strategies:

1. **Stop and swap.** This involves becoming aware of negative or unhelpful thoughts. As these register in your mind, say "STOP" and swap the negative thought for something constructive or positive. This can work well if you have a recurring negative thought or worry. For example, "I always miss close putts" could be replaced with instructional self-talk such as "In the

hole." "I always snap hook my drive at the 5th" could be replaced with "Down the middle."

2. **Embrace and replace**. Some people get overwhelmed and cannot manage to control their negative thoughts. At these times, they can feel like they are failing, which undermines confidence even more. To deal with this it will be easier to embrace rather than to try to stop negative unhelpful thoughts. For example, you may be playing on a windy day and notice your self-talk is, "I hate the wind. I never play well in these conditions." Now, instead of trying to stop the thought, acknowledge it and seek to apply a more constructive approach. It's even better if you can add a bit of humor. For example, "Windy day, but I can play so I'm here to stay!" This jingle should bring a smile to your face.

3. **Lock and block**. This is where you identify some motivational self-talk that you can use to anchor your thoughts. These are positive messages that you can lock into your head and repeat to block out negativity. I have used a variety of lock and block strategies since I started playing golf and find them really helpful.

Here are a few examples that I utilize:

- In my head, I recite the lyrics from a strong, positive song that I like when I feel unsettled. A song like "The Greatest" by Sia works well for me.

- I wear a silicone bracelet or have a piece of tape with a few inspirational words on it around my wrist. During the round, I will focus on the words and repeat them to myself.

- I use a laminated card with helpful keyword cues. When I need to focus, have self-belief and block negative self-talk I will take the card from my pocket and study it. This works well when walking between longer shots or holes.

Why not choose some song lyrics, words, or phrases that are meaningful to you and routinely introduce them to your game? I'm confident you will quickly notice positive improvements in your focus, demeanor, attitude, and mindset, but beware of overdoing it. In my experience, having two of the above strategies prepared for any given day is better than relying on one. However too much self-talk, either good or bad, can be an unhelpful distraction.

IMAGERY

A common characteristic of great athletes in all sports is their ability to use images to support and enhance their performance. Consequently, it should be no surprise that visualization is a fundamental part of the pre-shot routine of all great golfers.

Jack Niklaus said: "I never hit a shot, not even in practice, without having a very sharp, in-focus picture of it in my head. First, I see the ball where I want it to finish, nice and white and sitting up high on the bright green grass. Then the scene quickly changes, and I see the ball going there; its path, trajectory, and shape, even its behavior on landing. Then there is a sort of fade-out, and the next scene shows me making the kind of swing that will turn the previous images into reality."

Similarly, Jason Day explained that after completing two practice swings, he steps away from the ball, closes his eyes, and sees himself hitting the perfect shot. He stated: "When I close my eyes, I see a picture of myself. I visualize my swing and go back, and go through, and I see the ball land and how it goes, where it lands, and how it bounces. I make sure I don't hit the shot until I'm fully comfortable with the visual."

Imagery is not just about visualizing a situation. It ideally involves using all of your senses to see, hear, feel, smell, and taste the experience without it being the real thing. What follows is an example of imagery incorporating all of the senses:

> It's a hot summer's day and you are about to tee off to start your game. In your mind's eye, you see a well-flighted drive to the center of the fairway. You feel the sensations in your hands as you grip the club, your feet as you distribute your weight,

your hips, shoulders, and arms as you swing through the ball. You tune into the crisp, clean sound of the club face contacting the ball. You smell the freshly cut grass in the surrounding environment and notice a salty taste on your lips due to light perspiration.

Becoming proficient at imagery that engages all of your senses takes time and practice. For some people it may come more easily. As you are developing this skill, be patient and gentle with yourself. You will never get good at something you do not enjoy, so start slowly with one sense and have fun with it. Once you have developed a single sense, see what you can add next.

When you visualize a golf shot, many of the areas of your brain that will be engaged when performing the actual shot are activated. Research involving imagery in a number of sports, including golf with beginners,[3] has shown that imagery combined with actual practice improves performance more than practice alone. Consequently, it should not be considered as only in the domain of professional golfers. Instead, it should be considered an essential tool that can benefit golfers of all ages and abilities.

Personally, when I am playing golf, I find my imagery usually involves visualization and kinesthetic senses, so I work with that. When I am away from the golf course, I sometimes practice imagery by sitting or lying down in a quiet place with my eyes closed. It is important that I am fully relaxed and have no time constraints. I choose a hole that I played poorly during my game and visualize it over and over the way I want to play it next time. In five minutes, I will engage as many senses as I can. I cannot tell you the number of times that this simple imagery activity has paid dividends for me. The next time I am at the hole, I have been successfully imagining it is as if I am on autopilot. Without hesitation, I commit to and execute the exact shot I have repeatedly played in my mind. It is a great feeling and not only gives me confidence in my game, but also in the value of imagery.

The following table identifies general and specific types of imagery that can be used to motivate and focus your mind.

Type	Imagery Functions	
	Motivation	Cognition
Specific	Goal-oriented. Imagining oneself achieving a specific goal.	Skill development. Imagining oneself performing a specific skill, such as driving or putting.
General	Arousal-focused. Imagining oneself either in a relaxed, calm, or psyched mode. Mastery. Imagining oneself succeeding in difficult situations.	Strategy-based. Imagining one's game plan or how to play on the course to achieve the best score.

Table 1: Imagery Types and Functions

Here are some strategies to apply the different types of imagery in your game:

1. **Specific goal-oriented imagery**. This is a good place to start your imagery practice. Maybe you want to get your handicap into single figures or be chosen to

represent your club, state, or country. With your specific goal in mind, find a quiet place, close your eyes, and for a few minutes every day, live your dream. A great time to do this is before you fall asleep at night and as the first thing you do after waking up in the morning.

For this to have the optimal benefit, you should set a SMART goal. Refer to Section 1 on creating the right headspace if you need a refresh. Look closely at the A (Achievable) and the R (Relevant) aspects of SMART goals, so that your dream is within the realms of possibility and not simply wishful thinking. This daily imagery practice can then serve to motivate you, particularly with your training, and to boost your spirits if you have any setbacks, such as illness or injury.

2. **Arousal-focused imagery skills**. This is really helpful if you are a nervous or tense person and find it hard to settle into your round of golf. Imagine yourself as calm, relaxed, and in control. Align your imagery with the mindful practices discussed earlier in this section. Start practicing this imagery with eyes closed for a few minutes each day in a comfortable environment, away from the course. Once you feel well connected to your imagery, start to integrate it into your pre-game routine before you tee off. Next, bring it into your pre-shot and post-shot activities during practice. Then, when

you feel it is comfortably embedded, bring it into play all the time when you are on the course.

3. **Specific skill development imagery.** This can help you better connect with yourself and your game. Which area(s) of your game need attention? The answer may be obvious, or you may need to talk with your coach or mentor. Sometimes reviewing your statistics will help too. Your goal is to convert your weaknesses into strengths, but to do that you need to see your faults as rough diamonds in need of polishing and not as worthless rocks.

Choose <u>one</u> aspect of your game to work on as a starting point. This is really important. Focus on the image you want to see in terms of the set up and execution of the shot. Once again start practicing this imagery with eyes closed for a few minutes each day in a comfortable environment away from the course. Your coach or mentor can guide you on what you should see, do, and feel with the shot. Incorporate as many of your senses as possible into your imagery. Once you feel well connected to your imagery, start to integrate it into your pre-shot routine. It is only when you have this specific skill imagery ingrained in your mind and game that you should move on to another skill. You will notice that when you have learned imagery for one skill, adding in other skills will be quicker and easier.

4. **General mastery motivation.** This is great for those shots that most challenge you or for shots where you hold any fear or dread. For example, you may have short-sided yourself and need to play out of a bunker onto a fast, down-sloping green. Your first thought is that it will be impossible to stop the ball anywhere near the hole. Why not give your brain something amazing to focus on and imagine yourself getting the ball out of the bunker and into the hole?

Realistically, you may make only one of these shots in every 100 attempts, but that is not the point. As Arnold Palmer said, "Always make a total effort even when the odds are against you." Sow the seed of possibility in your mind so that you can commit 100 percent to the shot. You will surprise yourself how well you do because you remove all fear and create a possibility that is so exciting to pursue that you can forget what might be hinging on it.

With this type of imagery, see yourself overcoming impossible odds and always succeeding. Even when you don't manage to quite pull it off, you will usually have played a decent shot and will feel happy and relieved to limit any significant damage to your score for the hole.

If you cannot seem to easily imagine yourself pulling off grand feats on the golf course, try substituting in someone else. Choose your favorite player and in your mind see them playing the shot. What did they do? How did they do it? Allow yourself to become that person and play a shot to be proud of. Some people find the vicarious experience easier to see in their mind. Do whatever it takes to help you decide, commit, and execute the shot with confidence.

5. **Strategy-based imagery.** This is something to focus more closely on once your imagery skills in other areas have evolved. It is particularly useful for highly proficient amateurs or professional golfers. As part of their preparation, they will usually play one or more practice rounds and spend time walking the course to take in the layout, identify any hazards, and analyze areas to play to or stay away from. This can assist in developing imagery associated with course navigation that helps an individual to focus on how to structure and play their round.

In general, one of the common issues when people are learning imagery is an expectation that their imagery should be completely formed and flawless to be successful. They are disappointed if their imagery is not like a Steven Spielberg movie when in reality, some days you will find it easier than others. My advice to you regarding the use of imagery is to start small and see what happens. Do not be discouraged if your mind's hard drive is not always providing crystal clear images, or if you only manage to activate one or two of your senses at the beginning.

Self-compassion is critical as you are developing your imagery skills because it will take time and effort. Everyone is different, so be prepared to take the time you need to get the results you want. The payoff is that the stronger your imagery, the more effectively you will be able to concentrate, control your nerves, adapt to changes, and most importantly, embrace and enjoy the challenges you face on the golf course.

Summary

In this section, we started with a focus on the value of identifying your learning preferences. This will help make your learning more efficient and effective. We then discussed strategies to assist you to develop and utilize mindfulness, concentration, positive self-talk, and imagery skills. Start off with the skill or skills that you feel most comfortable with and build up your repertoire from there. As you get better at integrating the skills into your practice, you will be well positioned to embed them when competing.

REFLECTIVE QUESTIONS

Based on this section's information, you may find it helpful to write down some answers to the following questions:

1. What are my learning preferences? (For help in identifying your preferences, you can access and complete the VARK for athletes at http://vark-learn.com/)

2. How can I utilize knowledge of my learning preferences to help myself make progress with my game?

3. How would I rank my ability in the four skill areas of mindfulness, concentration, self-talk, and imagery? Use a scale where 1 is the strongest area at the moment and 4 is the weakest area.

4. What is one thing I can do to make my strongest skill area even better?

5. What is one thing I can do to start improving in my weakest skill area?

Section 3
Performance: Let It Happen

"On the first tee I kept telling myself, ' Trust yourself; you can do it.'"

—Annika Sorenstam

To consistently perform to the best of your ability on the golf course, you should stick with the routines you have developed and refined over time and learn to quickly review and accept whatever happens. This will require more in the way of mental rather than physical stamina, particularly to keep your emotions in check when things are going well, or poorly. In this section we explore the impact of the conscious, subconscious and unconscious mind, discuss the importance of self-trust, skill development, and being able to accept and quickly move on from mistakes.

How does your mind work?

Despite a lack of experimental evidence, a three-component model involving the conscious, subconscious, and unconscious is often used to explain how the mind works. This was popularized by Sigmund Freud (1856-1939) who described the mind being like an iceberg.

The conscious mind is the part of the iceberg that sits above the water line. It contains thoughts, feelings, and memories within one's awareness. It is in charge of one's thinking while also directing focus, movements, and speech. The conscious mind enables us to use our imagination, which explains why imagery can be a valuable aid to performance. The subconscious mind is the part of the iceberg that is submerged below the water but is still visible. It allows us to recall what we need and controls non-verbal communication, breathing, and automated movements. The subconscious mind will generate emotions and feelings that you think about. The unconscious mind is the part of the iceberg that is invisible below the water line. It is a reservoir holding past experiences, deep-seated emotions, and memories that may be repressed due to trauma or simply forgotten because they are no longer important.

Let's consider how the three-component mind model works when two golfers face the same scenario but get very different outcomes. In this scenario, the ball is sitting on the fairway about 110 yards (100 meters) from a large elevated green with greenside bunkers at the front on both the left and right. The flag is positioned in the center of the green, and there is a moderate headwind.

> Golfer 1 looks at the flag position, the lie of the ball, the line he wants to take for the shot, and the distance. He factors in the breeze and chooses his club for the shot (conscious mind). He goes through his pre-shot routine and just before he plays the shot, his last thought is, "Don't hit it into the bunker" (subconscious mind). Next, he executes the shot (unconscious mind).

> Golfer 2 looks at the flag position, the lie of the ball, the line she wants to take for the shot and the distance. She factors in the breeze and chooses her club for the shot (conscious mind). She goes through her pre-shot routine and just before she plays the shot, her last thought is "Middle of the green, straight at the flag" (subconscious mind). Next, she executes the shot (unconscious mind).

So, what were the outcomes of the two shots? Golfer 1 hit his ball into the bunker, while golfer 2 landed her ball pin high, close to the flag. You may recollect similar experiences when you have been playing golf and immediately before execution of a shot, a thought that came into your mind had a positive or negative effect on the outcome.

How does this happen? The subconscious and unconscious parts of your mind are servants to the conscious mind and will act on the information given. In the case of Golfer 1, the last thought passed to the subconscious was about the bunker. The individual was giving a direction to himself to hit it there. As for Golfer 2, she thought about the outcome she wanted and was able to execute it. These outcomes are not coincidental. They reflect the power of the mind and how it can affect performance.

Here are some tips to help you to make the best use of your mind:

1. **Become a reliable witness to your performance.** Given your pre-shot routine becomes automated, it is possible that over time you may vary it without being consciously aware of doing so. This can explain why the consistency of your ball striking can change even though you think you are doing everything the same. Consequently, you must learn to pay particular attention to both the physical and mental cues of your pre-shot routine and make sure you repeat them accurately.

2. **Identify thoughts and actions that can focus your conscious mind.** To do this, you should utilize the mindfulness activities, concentration, positive self-talk,

and imagery techniques discussed in the previous section.

3. **Think and see success rather than failure.** It can be difficult to narrow your focus of attention, particularly if you are nervous as you stand ready to play a golf shot. However, when faced with any shot, always think of the outcome you want and plant that seed firmly in your mind rather than thoughts or images of what you don't want.

4. **Accept that you will not always get it right.** It may be that there are too many thoughts racing through your mind, or you get stuck with some negative self-talk and fail on your execution of a particular shot. When this happens, it is important to recognize everyone makes mistakes. The best thing you can do is move on; otherwise you risk creating an issue in your subconscious that can affect subsequent shots. If you make a recurring mistake, such as mishitting chip shots, the belief that you are not good at chipping can become entrenched in your unconscious causing a significant longer-term problem.

BUILDING SELF-TRUST

Self-trust can be a fragile thing. Sometimes you have it and your game feels solid. Other times, like when you have been working on your technique, or after you come back from a break due to illness or injury, self-trust can be elusive.

When you lack self-trust, you can view your entire game as a mess and feel like giving up. Alternatively, you may try to come up with some quick fixes as you analyze and correct faults while you are playing. This is something that would best be left until you get some coaching or the next time you are on the practice range. Yet, sometimes we find it hard to resist and end up subjecting ourselves to paralysis by analysis. If you get too caught up thinking, there will be limited to zero value added when it comes time to play your next shot. The outcome is usually always the same—not good!

To build self-trust you should:

1. **Get comfortable with who you are and how you play the game.** Avoid comparing yourself, your swing, or how far you hit the ball to others. Instead, work on identifying what makes you special and unique—own your strengths.

2. **Challenge yourself to discover your capability.** If you are aspiring to be a golf professional, this may translate to spending hours and hours learning to shape shots on the practice range. If you are a novice, you may start by choosing your favorite club and simply working on your grip and posture, your set up,

swing drills, or ball striking. Think big but start small so you set goals that are challenging but achievable.

3. **Show courage under pressure.** You may get the yips with putts from a certain distance or have a difficult shot to play from a bunker to try and save par. In these circumstances, every time you feel anxiety or fear, embrace the challenge and say to yourself, "I love it. I love it. I love it." View it as a positive learning experience and over time, you will be surprised at how you enjoy the challenge and become more successful under pressure.

4. **Take responsibility for your game and build resilience.** Golf is an individual pursuit, and when things are not going well, it is easy to blame something or someone else. Instead, take charge of your game and accept responsibility for the good, bad, and ugly shots that you play on any given day. Learn from your mistakes. By doing so, not only will you develop your game, but also you will develop as a person. When you find a way to score even though your game is not in great shape, you will feel a real sense of accomplishment often more meaningful than when you seem to score effortlessly.

Sometimes you will be faced with a shot that makes you feel uneasy. It may be that the lie of the ball is poor, the landing spot looks tight, or the distance required puts you between clubs. For times like that, I have a self-talk ritual that involves repeating the words "head-heart-hands". This ritual helps me mentally prepare for and commit to the shot I need to play. Because each word has a particular meaning, for me the strategy is very effective for promoting self-trust:

1. **Head**. This refers to my decision-making process. When I say it, I am affirming to myself that I have made the right decision.

2. **Heart**. This reminds me of the need to make a 100 percent commitment to the shot.

3. **Hands**. This refers to the fact that I hold the golf club and thus, the outcome in my own hands.

You may want to utilize this ritual or come up with your own example that can help you to focus, commit to, and execute difficult shots. Ultimately, when you fully trust in your ability, you will be comfortable to manage the golf course according to your game. You will not hesitate because of your poor shots or get caught up in how others choose to play. Once a decision has been made, you will play each shot with full conviction. You will expect every shot to be 'a great shot,' but even if it is not, you will have the ability to quickly move on.

As a consequence of self-trust, you will exhibit a high degree of self-reliance. So, when a mistake is made, you will accept responsibility for it. You will not waste energy blaming your equipment or distractions in the external environment. You will learn from your mistakes and not dwell on your faults.

Subsequently, anyone with a great golf mind is aware of the importance of consolidating both the physical and mental aspects of their game to build self-trust. The amount of time required will vary depending on one's current level and aspirations, but importantly, self-trust is critical for golfers at all levels of ability.

Skill Development

If you are thinking about anything while you are swinging your golf club, you are going to achieve a suboptimal result. A major objective of practicing your golf swing is so that it becomes automated. We have already discussed how the collaboration, or lack thereof, between your conscious, subconscious, and unconscious mind can have an impact. We have also discussed the critical need to develop self-trust. Without this awareness and these practices, you will not be confident to automatically execute shots.

The basis for automation comes down to the processes associated with learning a new skill. Over many years, various authors have published work describing models of learning that are in stages from beginner to expert.

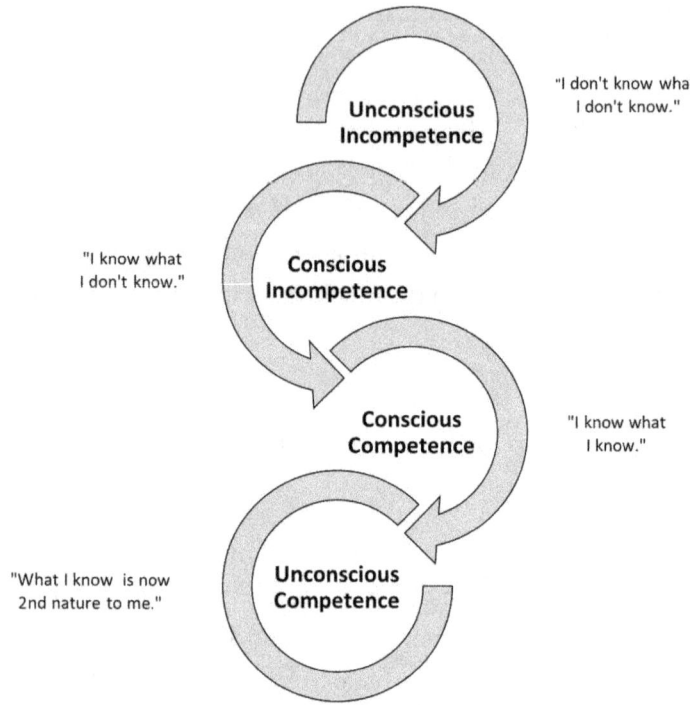

Figure 3: Stages in the Development of Competence

The most commonly referenced model[4] presents the development of competence using four stages:

1. **Unconscious incompetence.** This is where an individual does not know how to do something but may not recognize the extent of their deficit. In my work with junior golfers, sometimes this is evident when a novice youngster makes a comment that he/she will have a scratch handicap within a year or two. While the individual may have endless

enthusiasm, they are not yet aware of what is actually required to make such a dramatic transition. Improvement can certainly be rapid at the beginning, but the law of diminishing returns suggests that as one's handicap gets lower, the amount of effort required to make the desired progress increases exponentially.

2. **Conscious incompetence.** At this point, an individual has started to learn the skills required and quickly comes to the realization that they are perhaps not as good as they first thought. During this stage there is a massive amount of learning and the process of advancement will depend on an individual's commitment and effort, as well as the effectiveness of the teaching methods. Having a coach who can tailor the teaching to one's learning preferences will help a great deal. Also, being able to chunk the learning into small digestible bites will mean a learner maintains their motivation (even when they are struggling) and enjoys the process of learning.

3. **Conscious competence.** In the early phase of conscious competence, an individual may be better at describing the steps associated with performing a skill, rather than actually doing it. As they get better, they will be able to perform the skill reliably at will. Within this stage, individuals will demonstrate a wide variation in proficiency, but will be aware of what is required to

successfully perform the skill. The engagement in practice to improve performance is fundamental to develop high levels of conscious competence. However, as you will learn in Section 5 where we discuss making progress, it is not just that you practice, but how you go about it that really matters.

4. **Unconscious competence.** This is the point at which you can execute a particular skill without having to think about it. In golf, this is when a shot becomes second nature and you execute it automatically. You are confident in what to do and how you do it. Consequently, you trust that when you need to play a particular shot, it will happen, and you will get a good result. One of the challenges for individuals in this stage is avoiding slipping into bad habits. For example, if you have some muscle tightness, or a minor injury, you may adapt your swing without conscious awareness. If this is not bought to your attention so that you can fix it, you can quickly find the quality of your shot making falls away, and you are left scratching your head, wondering why. This is where the ability to accurately self-evaluate or to closely work with a helpful coach or mentor becomes really important.

Whatever your level of ability or swing mechanics, developing a safe, repeatable swing is necessary for consistent shot making. However, playing competitive golf to the best of your ability is not only about automation of your swing. On any given day, you need to be able to adapt to the environmental conditions as well as your playing partners. You need to be able to effectively use the range of clubs in your bag on demand. Also, you need to manage the mental side of your game which can ebb and flow over the four or more hours you are out on the course.

If you consider the range of factors associated with good performance, it can be helpful to reference your current level of skill against the four stages of learning. This is something that I have done to support my ongoing development. It has helped me to hold realistic expectations when I'm practicing and playing competitively.

For example, an absolute beginner (an individual in Stage 1) will mishit quite a few shots. A sound explanation for this is the fact the individual has yet to develop anything like a reliable swing. So, instead of getting frustrated and disappointed, it would be more productive if the individual could identify a favorite club and start building a more consistent swing with that club. As improvement occurs, the individual can leverage their perceived strength with their favorite club to using other clubs in the bag. This will make practice more enjoyable and productive.

Similarly, an individual who is progressing well in Stage 2 to 3 will find automation of some shots easier than others. This is to be expected, so rather than being disappointed because of overthinking shots, it would be more helpful if the individual worked on managing their pre-shot thinking and response to disappointment, which requires mental skills. After the round, the individual can discuss any physical and/or mental patterns they may have noticed with their coach or mentor and do some targeted work on the practice range.

For individuals who are well advanced in Stage 3 or 4, the process of improvement mostly involves refinement. Learning from mistakes will be part of the ongoing development.

In the context of an entire round of golf, the automated process of striking the ball accounts for only a fraction of total game time. Therefore, while it is important to develop appropriate routines that allow you to build and maintain self-belief, errors are inevitable. It is vital to learn how to process mistakes so they are not carried over into subsequent shots.

Accepting your mistakes

When a golfer is performing at their best, they usually feel relaxed, confident, and in control, playing each shot in a seemingly effortless way. The individual is fully immersed in what they are doing and has an ability to narrowly focus on the task at hand, has no fear of negative consequences, and sees the whole experience as fun. This is often referred to as being in a 'flow state' or 'in the zone.'

Even though you may be playing flawless golf, at some point it is likely you will make one or more errors. When this happens, how you deal with the situation will dictate whether you end up with a good, average, or poor score. There is no question that it can be difficult to accept your mistakes, particularly if you have spent countless hours training and have been hitting the ball well in practice.

When you get down on yourself it is important to find a way to give yourself an 'attitude transplant' so you can accept poor outcomes and move on. This is effectively giving yourself a 'kick in the pants,' a jolt into reality so you can pick up the task at hand. There are several ways you can do this, including:

1. **Distraction and refocusing techniques.** Choose both a physical and mental cue, such as tapping yourself on the thigh and saying, "Move on," or making a fist with your dominant hand and saying, "Let go." With repetition, these techniques can become really effective.

2. **Asking yourself a question.** This will give you something other than your mistake to think about and act on. For example, you can ask yourself, "What do I need to focus on right now?" or "Now what?" If you find yourself slipping back into the past, repeat the question.

3. **Giving yourself permission to vent.** This provides you with an internal rather than external outlet for your disappointment and frustration. Make sure you only allow yourself to vent for a defined period. It may be the next 10 steps you take, or the next three deep breaths. During this time, allow yourself to think and feel all of the negative emotions that are bottled up inside. At the end of your time, say something to yourself like "Times up, move on" or "Leave it." This can help you snap out of a negative funk, and with time, you can learn to have some fun with this approach.

We all aim for peak performance, which results from the convergence of our ability to deal with the demands of a situation and the opportunities that present themselves. If we consider two golfers with equivalent skill sets in match play competition, the one who is better at handling the pressure and capitalizing on any mistakes made by their opponent will come out on top. However, because the result is determined over 18 holes (or more if required) the acuity of the mind becomes crucial. Lapses in confidence and concentration are likely to have more impact on the outcome than physical fatigue. Therefore, the mind is a huge factor in determining how well things turn out.

At the end of the day we all make mistakes. No one is perfect, so beating yourself up every time you fail only serves to diminish your capability. The bottom line is that our mistakes provide us with the opportunity to learn and improve. While there is some value in doing a quick review (on course), the secret is being able to quickly reach acceptance of mistakes and move on. You will be much better served if you leave the detailed analysis until you are off the course when the pressure to score is not hanging over your head.

Summary

In this section, we started with a focus on how the mind works. We then explored building self-trust and skill development an essential aspect of effective automation of your golf swing. However, during a round of golf, at some point you are likely to face adversity, so you need the ability to quickly accept poor outcomes and move on.

From this point forward, when you set out to play a competitive round of golf, always hold onto good intentions. If things don't quite go as planned, learn how to manage your disappointment so that you give yourself the best chance of success rather than allowing yourself to be pulled off track.

REFLECTIVE QUESTIONS

Based on this section's information, you may find it helpful to write down some answers to the following questions:

1. How will I foster better collaboration between the three components of my mind?

2. What steps will I take to build self-trust despite adversity?

3. What stage am I in regarding my own skill development? How can I use this information to further my progress?

4. What strategy or strategies will I adopt to help myself move on from my mistakes?

Section 4
Pursuit: Enjoyment and Success

> *"I have really enjoyed every minute I have spent in golf...I couldn't wait for the sun to come up the next morning so that I could get out on the course again."*

—Ben Hogan

There is plenty of sports research that indicates individuals who enjoy what they do will show greater levels of enthusiasm and remain involved in their sport for longer than those who do not. This is important because optimizing your performance will require determination and perseverance, along with the ability to cope in both the good and bad times.

In this section, we will explore the benefits of positive emotional states on performance. In addition, we will identify some core values and discuss how focusing on inherent strengths can build character that underpins success and most importantly, enjoyment of the game.

POSITIVE PSYCHOLOGY

In 1998, Martin Seligman[5] introduced the domain of positive psychology. It focuses on helping individuals minimize pathological thinking to develop a sense of optimism towards life. Seligman has described the construct as "the scientific study of optimal human functioning that aims to discover and promote factors that allow individuals and communities to thrive."

The goals of positive psychology are to encourage acceptance of one's past, optimism about one's future, and a sense of contentment and well-being in the present. It is not simply promoting self-help using positive thinking and acknowledges that anxiety and fear are an integral part of the human experience.

Take the 'fight or flight' response as an example. When an individual perceives danger, stress hormones are released to prepare their body to either stay and face the threat, or to run away. This invokes both a physiological response including: reduced blood flow to the skin making an individual go pale, a dry mouth, dilated pupils, sweating, increased heart rate, respiratory rate, and muscle tension. From a psychological perspective, an individual may have a sense of clarity, take control, and adopt an aggressive response (fight). Alternatively, they could feel anxious, be overwhelmed with negative thoughts, and become powerless (flight).

How we respond in situations we perceive as stressful comes down to how we evaluate the threat. It would be great if we only had an extreme response when we were actually in serious danger, but it does not work like that. Some people are overcome with anxiety when they merely think about one of their fears. A stress response is activated for others when they are faced with public speaking or when in a large crowd. Everyone is different.

During a round of golf, it is normal to experience a mixture of emotions related to performance. When we are playing well, we are likely to feel happy and content with our game. We may be totally absorbed in the game and have no conscious awareness of any particular thoughts. However, if we start to focus on the outcome of a potentially great score and get distracted from what we need to focus on right now, we can quickly drop a few shots and then go on an emotional rollercoaster as we fight to get back on track.

Conversely, when we are in a negative headspace, every shot brings with it a degree of fear and trepidation: "How can I get this drive to stay on the fairway?" or "Am I going to hit my ball into the rough again?" or "I can't believe I've put my ball into another bunker!" If you get on too much of a downward spiral, it can be very difficult to see anything positive in your game. Before you know it all you can think about is finishing the game so you can get off the course. The end cannot come soon enough!

It is worthwhile to reflect on how you interpret good and bad situations on the golf course.

Do you have a well-balanced or more extreme negative response? Do you tend to catastrophize your poor shots? Do you dwell on all of the negatives associated with your play? Conversely, do you always look for the upside and find yourself thinking "Wow—it could have been so much worse." Research in positive psychology has shown that individuals who can maintain a positive emotional state will be more optimistic, derive greater levels of satisfaction from what they are doing, and be more creative problem solvers compared to those who adopt a negative emotional state. Whatever your approach, it is worth remembering that it is not what happens to you, but how you choose to deal with it that really matters.

Positive Emotions

Certain skills and characteristics are generally present in high achieving versus low achieving athletes. These include attributes like calmness, confidence, the ability to focus, optimism, setting challenging, but achievable goals, all with a sense of fun and enjoyment.

When you are performing poorly, it is hard to keep fighting when every part of your being is telling you to give up and go home. It may seem pointless trying to remain positive when nothing is working, and the level of disappointment increases with each shot. In my experience, this is when most people give up.

Whenever you concede to the negative or downside of things, you run the risk of taking little or no learning away from the experience. Human nature tells us that no one likes to experience any form of physical or emotional pain; we'll move away from it whenever possible. So, when you are disappointed and distressed during a round of golf, you are less likely to want to reflect on what happened, why it happened, and how to improve because you are hurting and just want to move on.

What many people fail to realize is that by adopting more positive emotions in a difficult situation, they can transform how they think, feel, and act. This takes courage, but can preserve confidence, rather than amplifying fear that more often than not results in failure. By learning to accept your mistakes as part of the journey, you can sift through the negative experiences to extract the fragments that provide you with the keys to your improvement. This reflective insight can serve you well both on and off the golf course, as you learn to build resilience and turn adversity into future success.

You may be feeling cynical and think that it is impossible to flip from negative to positive thinking. Or you may be a fatalist and think that it won't matter what you do because once you are in a rut, you won't be able to change anything even if you try. Maybe you have experience playing golf with 'doom and gloom' merchants who seem to perceive and interpret everything negatively. It may be the difficult pin positions, the strength of the wind, the speed of the greens, the length of the rough—the list could go on! Sometimes it seems that these individuals derive pleasure from continually expressing negative emotions, with no insight into the impact of their behavior on themselves or others.

In reality, you have the power to choose how you will view and respond to any situation that you find yourself in. If you choose to only see the downside, it should be no surprise that adopting a negative perspective more often leads to negative outcomes. This approach generally results in a lot of energy going out and nothing coming back. It's very frustrating and exhausting.

If you develop the capacity to reinterpret negative events, you can bring forth positive energy and maintain effort that affirms rather than undermines your confidence. Some people will use humor to break the stress cycle and that is fine. You will be better served if you choose coping mechanisms that offer you the opportunity to make the best of a bad situation.

> Imagine you are playing your third shot to the green on a par 5. The shot should be straightforward, but you make a poor swing and send the ball fast and hard through the green where it ends up in an awkward position in the rough. In this situation it is easy to entertain anger and disappointment by asking, "How could I have stuffed up a straightforward shot?" or "What was I thinking?"

There is no value added from consuming yourself with negative thinking because you can't undo what you have just done. What would be useful is to apply positive emotions to the task at hand. This at least helps you to focus your attention 'in the present' and bolsters your confidence. Repeating something like "I've got this." can help you to shift from dwelling on the problem (a poor prior shot), to focusing on the solution (what you need to do now).

Similarly, golf has a habit of exposing our underlying weaknesses and intensifying our fears—those kinks in our game that we either should be or are working on. Maybe it is your bunker play, putts from a certain distance, playing shots from the rough, or shaping shots on demand. The anxiety you feel is most likely caused by a lack of confidence stemming from limited practice, past bad experiences, or persistent negative self-talk. Some people can't help but beat themselves up! If we add to the mix an important competition and spectators watching your performance, it can become both overwhelming and disabling.

Golf has that uncanny ability of exposing our weaknesses. The discomfort and dread that we feel over a golf shot when we have so much hinging on it is palpable, and the cycle of fear of failure, leading to failure can rapidly become a self-fulfilling prophecy. It is easy to see why an individual might interpret a difficult situation as 'all downhill from here' and be willing to concede defeat. However, there is plenty of evidence that shows if an individual is willing to back themselves, to maintain self-confidence under pressure, he/she can succeed. Something that can really help is bringing forward positive emotions that encourage you to embrace the challenge.

Every time you find yourself facing a difficult shot, say to yourself, "I love this. I love this. I love this." What you are aiming to do is regulate your anxiety, so you do not allow your brain to continue to entertain the fear. Instead you are reprogramming yourself to see and embrace the opportunity in the threat. You will be amazed at how the shift in attitude can have a dramatically positive effect on your results. This is because by changing your thinking, you bring a can-do attitude and wholehearted commitment. Try it and see if you can learn to enjoy making the switch.

If you fail to adequately manage your anxiety, and you execute a poor shot, make another attempt to reframe the situation. For example, you may hate bunkers and find yourself with a difficult bunker shot to play to try and get up-and-down. The best-case scenario is you do a great bunker shot, and it goes in the hole. The worst-case scenario is you fail to get the ball out of the bunker.

There is no question that by failing to hit a good shot, you are placing yourself under more pressure. However, in the struggle you now face, you have even greater potential for learning, which is positive. Use that potential to double down and commit to the task. In doing so, when you clear the ball from the bunker, you are left with the opportunity to use the situation as motivation to turn a weakness into a strength. Perhaps now you'll commit to making that lesson you have been putting off with your coach, or you will schedule more time to practice.

Of course, no one likes to fail at anything. However, when you embrace failure and take some time to sift through the mess that is left behind, you will develop insight that ultimately helps you become stronger, more determined, better at your game, and better as a person.

Building Character

People of good character attract trust and respect from others through their words and actions; they can often ride the tide of success and failure equally well. These individuals exhibit self-belief, are honest, confident, and resilient, all of which positively influences those around them. In addition, they know what is important to them and establish core values that act as guiding principles in their life.

One of the great gifts afforded to those who play golf is the opportunity to learn and demonstrate positive character traits, particularly in difficult times. Such behavior can constructively shape a successful life both on and off the course. Golf legend Gary Player recognized this when he said: "To succeed in life, one must have determination and must be prepared to suffer during the process. If one isn't prepared to suffer during adversities, I don't really see how he can be successful."

We could brainstorm the character traits we each think are most important. If we did, I'm sure we would come up with dozens of examples. To get you thinking about important character traits that can be developed on the golf course, I have provided 10 examples in the following list. They are in no particular order but do reflect traits that I exemplify and try to foster in others, especially when playing the game. I would encourage you to create a list with your own examples. More importantly, I would like you to think about how you can contribute to building and shaping your own and the character of others when playing golf.

1. **Integrity**. There is a myriad of opportunities to encourage this trait in golf, the most obvious being related to keeping an accurate score card and dutifully following the rules of golf. In reality, people who choose to be dishonest on the golf course may get away with it because a great deal of self-monitoring is involved. However, if we can instill the importance of integrity very early in the development of a golfer, whether they are young or more mature, and provide them with education and support on the fundamentals, we can make it easier for them to do the right thing at the right time in the right way.

2. **Respect**. Golf can teach us multiple lessons about respect, including from the viewpoint of an individual, team, or club, and even from the game itself. Firstly, at an individual level it is important to arrive in plenty of time to warm up, wear appropriate attire, and be ready to cordially interact with one's playing partners before, during, and after the round. Secondly, you never know who is watching you. Individuals should note that not only will their behavior reflect on them, but also on any teammates and their club. Therefore, it is essential to show respect for others at all times. Thirdly, golf is a game that is bigger than the sum of the individuals who play it, so ultimate respect should be shown for

the game. This can be demonstrated by observing the rules and getting a better understanding of the history of the game, of your club, and those who have come before you.

3. **Creativity.** With 14 clubs and 18 holes to navigate in each round of golf, you have countless opportunities for creativity in how you choose to play the course. It is helpful if you can learn to see a shot before you play it (imagery) and get a feel for how to create the outcome you want. This is where golf can be as much an art as a science, and often as players advance in skill, their confidence to utilize their creativity flourishes and should be encouraged. Applying creativity to shot making will help you develop an all-around better game.

4. **Humility.** This is a trait that ensures we are courteous and considerate of the people around us. The best way to teach humility is by example, and the best time to teach it is during childhood. Individuals who are humble will be down-to-earth and demonstrate self-confidence without the need for cockiness. They will be content for others to discover their talents without the need to advertise them and will be open to listen and learn from those around them while showing consideration and respect. An individual with humility will be clear that their success has not only come from

their hard work, but also from the coaching, mentorship, support, and friendship of others.

5. **Commitment.** No one achieves their goals without focus, dedication, and commitment. To excel at golf takes time. An individual must develop reliable physical and mental routines to maintain consistent performance. Physical routines are easier to check, measure, and manage. Mental routines largely focus one's attention to subjective internal processes, which usually require considerable effort to establish and monitor. Success is dependent on unwavering commitment to the processes and structures that are put in place.

6. **Individuality.** All too often people prefer to fit in with the crowd. There is a level of comfort in being like everyone else, However, to optimize your potential, you should discover what works for you and seek to walk your own path. This requires courage but having a greater knowledge of oneself will bolster confidence. This can help you stand out in the crowd, which is highly beneficial if you want to develop a psychological advantage over others, or to demonstrate the special features that make you unique.

7. **Responsibility.** This is about taking ownership of one's thoughts, words, and actions. In golf, you need to make decisions, as well as act and deal with the consequences. Individuals who struggle to take control

of their destiny will often blame their caddy, equipment, or the environment. However, in reality, it is the player who executes the shot. As soon as that individual learns to stand up and accept that the buck stops with them, they will be better placed to improve their game because they will stop looking for excuses. Consequently, a willingness to take full responsibility for things within your control gives you a much greater chance of self-improvement and future success.

8. **Determination.** Even when we are not striking the ball to the best of our ability, we still want to play well. In these circumstances it takes a great deal of effort to play a solid round of golf, but it is possible with sheer determination. This is an attribute shown among great golfers who somehow manage to grind out a decent round even when they are not playing at their best. Consequently, showing determination in the face of adversity is admirable and a character trait well worth nurturing.

9. **Patience.** Golfers must demonstrate patience when dealing with slow pace of play or unexpected occurrences like a lost ball or waiting for an official to make a ruling. In addition, when an individual is feeling anxious, they will often speed up their physical and mental routines, which then affects their rhythm, timing, concentration, and focus. This can result in a dramatic fall-off in performance. Therefore, it is

important to demonstrate patience and self-compassion. There is no point in getting angry or more distressed when a sense of calm and control is the best antidote to the situation.

10. **Optimism.** This is about having positive expectations of future events. Without optimism an individual can lack energy and focus, creating insufficient effort. Since optimism can be taught, it makes sense for golfers to choose it over pessimism because not only does it create a positive vibe, but also it helps you to effectively process failure. Over 18 holes even the very best players will make mistakes. Therefore, the ability to be able to quickly accept an error and develop a plan to move on is essential. Furthermore, it is never much fun to spend long periods of time with pessimists. They tend to hold onto negativity and drain all that is good or enjoyable from a given situation.

Young people who are still developing can have their character positively shaped through lessons learnt playing golf. As we move into adulthood and later life, we have even greater potential and responsibility to (1) demonstrate good character; (2) share character building lessons with those around us; and (3) to actively keep shaping ourselves. Such action enables us to become a valuable role model who positively influences others, and in doing so, the gift we receive is a greater sense of well-being.

Whether you play golf as an amateur or a professional, if you are striving to get better, you are constantly a work in progress. While your physical potential has a defined ceiling as a consequence of maturation and aging, your psyche has enormous potential for ongoing development, so striving to continually build character can be a valuable part of that process.

A STRENGTHS-BASED APPROACH

We all have our strong and weak areas, and adopting a strengths-based approach is not about ignoring the parts of your game that let you down. Instead, it promotes a solutions-based focus and encourages individuals to recognize and use the resources they have to the best of their ability. In the first instance, that will mean focusing on the things you are good at and feel most confident doing.

A traditional approach to coaching a novice golfer will focus on the basic physical components for making a good swing. This includes addressing posture, grip, alignment, balance, body and shoulder rotation, along with club position at different points in the swing. This makes sense, but it takes an astute coach to be able to break down the components into digestible teaching chunks and then to tailor that information to each learner. An experienced coach will identify the high-priority areas and start there knowing that if they have chosen correctly, many minor issues will automatically resolve. However, providing just the right amount of information, in the right way, and at the right time requires a great deal of skill from the coach.

A strengths-based approach can provide a powerful way to accelerate learning and performance by aligning with an individual's natural strengths and personality, unlocking their energy and passion, and starting them from a place of comfort and confidence. Think about your game. How can you leverage your mental and physical strengths to improve the weaker areas of your game?

Let's consider an average amateur golfer as an example. It may be that their mind, not their physical prowess, is their greatest asset. This may be apparent when they say, "I have always been able to focus and concentrate really well." Consequently, it will be helpful to bring the attributes of commitment and concentration to improving in a weaker area like chipping. Getting the chipping technique right and learning how to control ball flight and distance takes time and practice. There will undoubtedly be challenges and setbacks along the way. However, by inherently focusing on their strengths, the golfer will bring good energy and effort that ultimately has the potential to make chipping another strength in their game.

You may be thinking, "Is it possible to overdo a focus on strengths?" The simple answer is yes—too much of a good thing does not necessarily provide you with the results you want. If you get so invested in your strengths, you may find the gap between your strengths and weaknesses gets further apart rather than closer together. If you apply your strengths in the wrong way or at the wrong time, you can expect poor outcomes. Similarly, if you become overconfident in doing things your way, you may filter out valuable information and then wonder why your progress has stalled. These effects can easily be moderated by building self-awareness and getting appropriate feedback from a coach or mentor.

A strengths-based approach is equally relevant for highly skilled amateur and professional golfers. These individuals have many strengths and higher levels of self-awareness than an average golfer. However, because they are continually fine-tuning their skills, there is a tendency towards perfectionism, meaning they are more likely to get fixated on their weaknesses. In principle, this seems to be a good idea, but it can result in a very narrow focus and high level of intense self-criticism. At times, like when learning stalls, or during a form slump, these individuals may lose confidence and enjoyment for the game. The result being a decline in motivation and performance.

If you are a high-level performer, it is important to see the big picture in terms of your overall ability and how much you have developed in different areas over time. When you are working hard to improve a specific skill, remember to validate your strengths on a regular basis. This will help you to put things into perspective. Next, focus on your sensory preference strengths and transfer this awareness and capability to the physical or mental skills you are currently working on.

The intended outcome for individuals using a strengths-based approach is to become creative problem solvers who are confident and self-sufficient, especially when under pressure. This does not mean a good caddy, coach, and support team are not needed, but rather that these aides add value to an already confident, self-contained package.

Based on the information provided, think about how you can become better at leveraging your strengths to improve your golf game. By doing so, you will be able to build from a more solid base while maintaining your energy and enthusiasm for the work ahead. The good thing is that you have nothing to lose from adopting a strengths-based approach, and you potentially have a great deal to gain.

Summary

In this section, you were introduced to positive psychology, and we discussed the benefits of positive emotions on performance. We also identified examples where golf can be beneficial for building character and explored the concept of adopting a strengths-based approach to improving your game.

Whether you are an amateur or professional golfer, if you want to improve your game, it is essential that you positively embrace the challenges you face and enjoy the journey. In doing so, success will be more likely, and fun will be assured.

REFLECTIVE QUESTIONS

Based on this section's information, you may find it helpful to write down some answers to the following questions:

1. When playing golf, how do I respond physically and mentally when under pressure?

2. What are three things I can do to improve my responses under pressure?

3. What character traits do I think can be developed by playing golf?

4. When playing golf, how can I actively shape my own character and the character of others?

5. What are the physical and mental strengths I bring to the game of golf?

6. How can I leverage my strengths to improve my game? Who can help me?

Section 5
Progress: Quality Versus Quantity

"My three keys to success: One, work hard. Two, be your own person. And three, have a passion for what you're doing."

—Juli Inkster

For anyone who has developed a passion for golf, the quest to improve is a constant. For a budding professional, this will equate to hours on the practice range each day refining and consolidating technique. For the average amateur golfer, it will be more about occasional practice and lessons, or buying new equipment to fine-tune their game.

It is easy to assume that the more you practice, the better you will become; however, this is a misconception. In this section, we will discuss the benefit of keeping things simple, explore how to practice, and consider how an action-learning approach can help you progress. You will come to appreciate that for those with a great golf mind, it is not so much about what they do, but how they go about it that matters.

THE KEEP IT SIMPLE SERIOUSLY (KISS) PRINCIPLE

In the 1970s, Kelly Johnson, a lead aircraft engineer at Lockheed, coined the phrase "Keep it simple stupid," and since that time, others have come up with a number of variations on the original, including my own iteration that I will discuss further.

Conceptually, golf is a really simple game. Your goal is to get a small ball to fall into a hole marked by a flagstick in as few shots as possible. The number of holes you will play is pre-determined, and a match committee will provide direction on the format and scoring method. This can make things a little more complicated. However, in essence, the aim of the game is straightforward.

What starts out as a simple concept becomes more complex when you have 14 clubs, a variety of golf balls with different features, and every course design is different. Then overlay the time of day, weather conditions, and the amount of time spent on course, which can also have significant impact. Lastly, but most importantly, consider the physical and mental attributes of the golfer. Age, experience, fitness or infirmity, attitude, motivation, concentration ability, and skill level all come into the mix. Consequently, the game provides many challenges, so much so it is unusual to find the same person announced as the competition winner each week.

For an individual to learn to consistently manage their game and the conditions, it makes sense to keep things as simple as possible. Nancy Lopez, one of the greatest female golfers of all time acknowledged this when she said, "The simpler I keep things the better I play." Think about a time when your own game imploded. Did you try hard to fix it and end up playing worse rather than better? You may have got involved in too much analysis and then not been able to execute your swing freely. You may have abandoned your swing or game plan altogether due to lost confidence. The reality is that when your game starts to slide, you need to be able to stabilize the situation. The best way to do this is to pare it back to simple thoughts and actions that give you the greatest likelihood of success.

When your game has gone off, it is easy to become erratic in both your thoughts and actions. Often the results are overcomplicating things and making poor decisions. This only serves to drag your game to an even lower point. For example, imagine you 3-putted the last hole and are still disappointed about it. The next hole you are to play is a par 5. Your drive goes into the rough and you are obstructed from playing a full shot toward the hole. As you weigh up your options you see that (1) you could chip it out and take your medicine; (2) you could play a low flat shot with a half swing in the hope of progressing the ball forward 100 yards (90 meters); or (3) you could do a 'Hail Mary' hit and hope shot.

When you are not thinking clearly, the temptation is to choose option 3. You may be thinking irrationally, with inner talk like this: "I can't afford to drop another shot so I have to go for this." Truthfully, you will drop at least one shot if you fail to pull off option 3. Backing yourself to be successful on a low percentage shot shows courage, but based on the game you are playing today, a good outcome is unlikely. If you keep it simple, you will choose option 1. Get the ball back in play and then focus on how you can get the ball up-and-down.

To make progress in the game, remember the importance of keeping your game plan and golf shots simple and sound. Focus on doing the basics really well and on making good decisions that ensure you choose to play shots that offer you the highest percentage of success. This will be critical when you are under the most pressure, or you are not striking the ball well.

When practicing and competing it is also important to have reliable decision-making and pre-shot routines. It helps when these processes are systematic and well-practiced, making things simple. Something else to consider involves developing a consistent preparation process for playing days. For an amateur golfer, this could mean getting gear ready the night before and deciding when to arrive at the golf club before the game. Once at the course, it could include completing a consistent warm up and any post-game practice or activities.

Dealing with the schedule of a professional golfer is more complex, so developing strategies to manage the range of commitments can be really helpful. This will involve establishing a plan for each event. The plan will address things like travel, food and hydration needs, sleep, practice and warm up routines, playing times, post-game activities, social engagements, media, and any other commitments.

Ultimately you want to make the activities you engage in to practice, prepare for, and play competitive golf orderly and purposeful. The aim is to have efficient and effective processes that enable you to feel comfortable and in control. This gives you a clearer headspace and that will help you to focus on the right things, in the right way, at the right time.

Deliberate practice

Over the last 25 years, Anders Ericsson and colleagues[6] have presented a great deal of research related to expert performers in sports, the arts and science. They claim that it is not simply engagement in practice that differentiates good performers from experts, but how these individuals conduct their practice.

The term deliberate practice refers to the systematic and purposeful engagement in a number of activities to improve performance. There has been some controversy in recent years about the extent to which deliberate practice accounts for the variation in performance of elite versus non-elite athletes.[7] However, it is worth considering how deliberate practice might assist you to make progress with your own performance.

The six deliberate practice components include;

1. **Planning**. This relates to making the best use of your time. It is an obvious strategy for improvement, so commit to making a clear plan and stick to it. This will ensure you avoid wasting practice time. Sometimes I notice golfers who appear to be mindlessly hitting ball after ball on the driving range with no obvious plan or purpose. This repetition may build confidence to strike a golf ball, but it does not automatically transfer onto the golf course where the conditions are variable and

the pressure to perform on demand is real. For those who have significant commitments outside of golf, planning your practice sessions is critical to ensure you can optimize your effort. Decide how much time you have and then break your session into focused sections. It may be a few different putting or short game drills. Make sure you set process and performance goals that will motivate and keep you on task.

2. **Well-defined and important tasks.** There is no value in practicing the wrong things or practicing in the wrong way as you can propagate problems and then wonder why you are not reaping the rewards of all your hard work. Your coach or mentor can help you to identify the main areas you need to focus on. Alternatively, based on recent performances you can probably identify one or more of these areas for yourself. The challenge is to be specific about exactly what aspect(s) of a skill you need to improve and then seeking to do this in a systematic and 'real world' way involving the integration of both physical and mental skills. This will ensure you make the best use of your time.

3. **Opportunities to practice.** This is not just about scheduling time for practice but considering where you practice, if you practice alone or with others, and how you practice so that you include some activities where

you have to perform under pressure. Your practice routine can get stale when it is the same repeated sequence each week. Changing venues, practicing alone and with different people, and setting milestones for each session can keep things fresh and interesting. Think creatively in terms of how you can make the most of your opportunities to practice. Sometimes I will make a time to play a practice round of 9 or 18 holes with others and set some specific performance goals. I will decide in advance on a reward or penalty if I meet or fail to meet my goals. This serves to motivate me and at the same time puts me under some pressure to perform. It also makes practice more fun. If you are going to use a reward-penalty system, make sure that both options are things that you actually like, want, or need to enhance your overall development, otherwise this approach can become counterproductive.

4. **Good supervision and feedback.** Building a good relationship with a coach or mentor who can provide you with quality teaching and give you constructive feedback is important. However, you also need to become an accurate witness to your own performance so that you are confident to adjust your training and game plan, as and when required. If you become too dependent on others it will be difficult to build a solid and consistent game where you are self-sufficient.

If you find it useful to ask a friend or playing partner for feedback, make sure they have something specific to focus on and are clear about your expectations. This discussion should occur after, not during the round. It is a strategy I have found useful to employ with junior golfers. Together, we will identify one or two general areas for them to work on during a round. These are never technique related as that is something for them to work on at the practice range with their coach. However, there are areas related to etiquette, mental skills, and professional behavior that can readily be addressed. For example, it may be reducing the number of practice swings before making a shot, walking with purpose to their ball between shots or maintaining positive body language throughout the round. I will prime the junior golfer and their playing partner/observer, usually an adult, on the plan and expectations. At the end of the round, I seek feedback from the observer and then hold a debrief discussion with the junior golfer. This approach has proven to be a win-win for all concerned as it directly supports progress in the game, as well as building and shaping of character that was discussed in the previous section.

5. **Conscious reflection.** This involves thinking about one's actions and the consequences and planning to improve. From a golf perspective, this can be a valuable process to employ on a shot-by-shot basis, as well as at the end of your round. However, it depends

on one's ability to accurately self-evaluate, and it requires an individual to be able to quickly accept both good and bad outcomes and move on.

In my experience, the ability to consciously reflect is not always related to the skill level of the golfer. However, elite performers will generally spend more time in conscious reflection at the end of a game and will develop the capability to do this to a high level. This will enable very detailed analysis that can assist in identifying physical errors and mental lapses which can then be addressed.

6. **Motivation and endurance.** To improve, you need a high level of motivation to practice and refine your physical and mental skills over time. While some individuals may have natural ability, allowing them to pick up certain skills more easily than others, ultimately there are no shortcuts. Once you decide on your outcome goal(s), you will need to put appropriate process and performance goals in place and be willing to do the work required to achieve them. It is inevitable that you will encounter setbacks along the way. It may be injury, illness, or other life events that shift your focus away from golf for a period of time. Having a high level of endurance enables you to push through any difficulties when you inevitably encounter ups and downs. In addition, having a good support network around you will be invaluable.

Deliberate practice affirms the importance of building on the quality of one's practice, rather than focusing solely on the quantity. This is especially positive for those who have limited time to train but have unlimited enthusiasm for the game. In preparation for the next time you go to practice on the driving range, or to work on your short game, take a few minutes now to think about how you can optimize the quality of your practice to make the progress you desire.

CONTINUOUS QUALITY IMPROVEMENT (CQI)

Imagine you have decided you want to improve your game, and you take a few lessons. After a number of hours of coaching and practice, you are encouraged when you notice improvement. However, once you get into a competitive round, you find you quickly revert to your old habits. The reality is that the process of making improvement is not easy.

Some people will practice what they think are the areas they need to work on and track their handicap as an objective measure of improvement. However, given that your handicap is determined by averaging a defined number of the *best* rounds you have played, it does not provide you with important information for quality improvement purposes. What you actually need as a quality improvement measure is a detailed analysis of how you played during the really poor rounds. This will point you to the areas you should prioritize. In the words of Colin Powell, American statesman and retired 4-star army general, "There are no secrets to success. It is the result of preparation, hard work, and learning from failure."

Committing to a CQI process that guides you on what to practice and how to practice is the obvious route to progress. It will provide you with clear direction and focus that helps you fine-tune your physical and mental skills. This is confirmed if you look closely at the inner workings of any successful company. You will notice that quality improvement processes are utilized to monitor and improve systems and methods. The same approach can work for you.

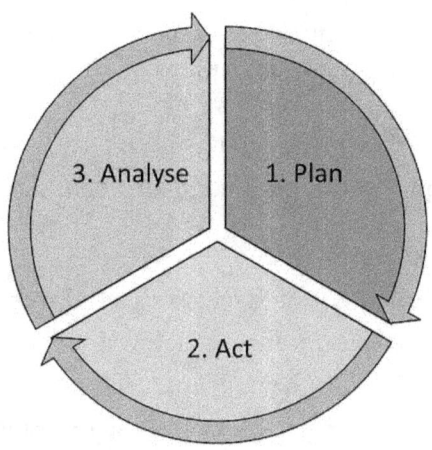

Figure 4: Plan-Act-Analyze Continuous Quality Improvement Cycle

The steps of Plan-Act-Analyze provide a simple CQI cycle you can follow. If one of your performance goals is to improve the accuracy of your drives in competition, you could work through the three-steps in the following way:

1. **Plan.** Decide how you will measure your performance and over what period. You could calculate your driving accuracy from a defined number of consecutive attempts and also rate the quality of each drive. Specifically, if you hit your drive a good distance and land on the fairway, score yourself an A grade. If you hit a good distance but land in playable rough or a bunker, score yourself a B grade. If you hit a playable ball but a poor distance, score yourself a C. Finally, if you hit the drive into an unplayable position, score yourself a D grade. The grading of both quantity and quality will provide you with information that may highlight potential issues and solutions that come under consideration in the Analyze phase.

2. **Act.** In this phase you will collect your drive data according to the timeframe and conditions you have set.

3. **Analyze.** Once you have collected the data, you need to review your findings to determine the next steps. It may be that you have 70 percent accuracy, but your poor drives are mostly a B or a D grade. This may focus your attention toward course management and also mental and technical areas for practice. After some work to improve in these areas, you can repeat the Plan-Act-Analyze cycle.

This action-learning cycle can be applied to one or more physical and mental skill areas of your game. By following the three-step process, you will be well on the way to greater levels of consistency and be able to consolidate your game. Earlier in this section I discussed the KISS principle and my advice is that your CQI process should reflect your goals and level of commitment. There is not much point in asking someone to collect detailed statistics as if they were a high-level amateur or professional if they are not willing to make a sustained effort to improve their game. The process of collecting the information will be onerous unless the individual starts to see how the data is helping them to develop their overall game. Similarly, if you aspire to become or are a professional, it is important that your plan, in particular deciding on the data to collect, will provide a sufficient level of detail to allow in-depth analysis.

Take some time to reflect on how and when you can put a CQI process in place to progress your game. Make sure it addresses both physical and mental components and enlist the help of a coach or mentor to support you. The bottom line is that anyone who truly wants to improve will put a CQI process in place because it will drive advancement toward their goals.

Summary

In this section, we discussed the value of keeping your practice and performance processes as simple as possible, explored the elements of deliberate practice and recommended putting a CQI process in place to help you progress.

Ultimately, you need to decide what you are prepared to do and the best ways to go about it. This will vary depending on your interest and motivation to improve as well as your current level of ability and expectations. Seek to make the best use of the coaching and educational resources that are available to you. However, in mapping out your pathway to improvement, make sure you choose options that you are willing to commit to and can have fun pursuing because in the words of Ralph Waldo Emerson, "Nothing great was ever achieved without enthusiasm."

REFLECTIVE QUESTIONS

Based on this section's information, you may find it helpful to write down some answers to the following questions:

1. How can I get better at self-evaluating my performance?

2. What human and other resources can I tap into to help me progress in the game?

3. What components of deliberate practice do I currently do well? Where can I improve?

4. In what area(s) of my game should I implement a CQI process?

Conclusion

Most mental skills books for golf adopt a narrow focus on teaching skills that target performance. This book has intentionally taken a broader perspective to enable you to see how the mind can be utilized holistically to have a positive impact on planning, preparation, performance, pursuit of enjoyment, success, and ultimately your progress in the game. By organizing things in this way, you have a big picture overview and can choose strategies within the cycle to make your own improvement plan.

The ideas and strategies discussed in this book reflect the roadmap that I have followed and utilize in my work supporting others. If you are ready to take charge of your game, decide in which area you will start. Review the different sections, in particular the tips and strategies discussed. Decide what resonates most strongly with you and start to build your capability from there. Use a strengths-based approach and deliberate practice to augment your learning. And while I would encourage you to dream big, start small.

You should now be in a prime position to create your own great golf mind. However, remember that the journey of self-improvement is a marathon not a sprint. You will need to be self-disciplined so that you can commit to and make sustainable change. Above all, you will need to be patient and self-compassionate. It takes time to alter old habits and form new pathways. There will undoubtedly be some frustration, and you will make mistakes, but the rewards will be worth the effort.

Depending on your golf aspirations, you may be happy to develop a limited repertoire of mental skills that you can comfortably integrate into your game. However, if you are driven to be the best you can be, work on developing your skills in all areas. This will expand your mental skill set and build resilience so that you can navigate the inevitable highs and lows of the game.

My final piece of advice is this: If you really want to become successful at playing **GOLF** then bring a **G**REAT attitude, **O**rganize your thoughts, **L**ove the process of learning, and most of all, have **F**un.

End Notes

[1] Neil D. Fleming and Colleen Mills. "Not Another Inventory, Rather a Catalyst for Reflection." *To Improve the Academy* 11, (1992): 137-144.

[2] Michael Bender and Maria Mercier. *Golf's 8 Second Secret: What Separates Golf's Greatest Champions*, Rochester NY: Lawless Publishing, 2016.

[3] Majid Brouziyne and Corinne Molinaro. "Mental Imagery Combined with Physical Practice of Approach Shots for Golf Beginners." *Perceptual and Motor Skills* 101, (2005): 203-211.

[4] W. Lewis Robinson. "Conscious Competency: The Mark of a Competent Instructor." *The Personnel Journal* 53, (1974): 538-539.

[5] Martin E. P. Seligman. "Building Human Strength: Psychology's Forgotten Mission." *American Psychological Association Monitor* 29, no. 1 (1998): 2.

[6] K. Anders Ericsson, Ralf T. Krampe, and Clemens Tesch-Rom. "The role of deliberate practice in the acquisition of expert performance." *Psychological Review* 100, no. 3 (1993): 363-406.

[7] Brooke N. Macnamara, David Moreau, and David Z. Hambrick. "The Relationship Between Deliberate Practice and Performance in Sports: A Meta-analysis." *Perspectives on Psychological Science* 11, no. 3 (2016): 333-350.

Acknowledgments

I would like to thank Vickey, Kihi and Zee for their unwavering support and encouragement throughout the journey of writing this book.

A big 'high five' to the junior girls at the Royal Fremantle Golf Club who provided me with the impetus to write this book. Each of you are unique and special. I hope that I can inspire you to follow your dreams. Keep being G-R-E-A-T!

To the members at the Royal Fremantle Golf Club, both ladies and men (you know who you are), who have always made me feel welcome. I will be forever grateful for your warm embrace and ongoing encouragement.

Thanks to Henry Stevens who as a coach and mentor continues to help me make progress in the game.

To Janine Northrop, Aruni Vaswani and Jen Owens who I have had the good fortune to meet and get to know playing the great game of golf. Each of you has been a positive and supportive influence and I am most thankful that our paths have crossed.

www.ingramcontent.com/pod-product-compliance
Lightning Source LLC
Chambersburg PA
CBHW072054290426
44110CB00014B/1676